MANGA MATHS MYSTERIES

THE KUNG FU PUZZLE

A Mystery with
Time and Temperature

by Melinda Thielbar
illustrated by Der-shing Helmer

LERNER BOOKS
LONDON • NEW YORK • MINNEAPOLIS

JOY
MEDINA

TOM
JOHNSON

ADAM
BREGMAN

STACY
LOWICKI

AMY
TSANG

SAM
CARTER

MICHELLE
CARTER

SIFU FAIZA

SIGUNG

BRIAN NARATA

SAM'S DAD

How do we measure **time**? We measure time in seconds, minutes, and hours. We read time on two kinds of clocks. An **analogue** clock has a minute hand and an hour hand and sometimes a second hand. A **digital** clock shows us the numbers for the hour and minutes.

How do we measure **temperature**? We measure temperature on a **thermometer**. There are two ways to measure temperature. In the UK and other parts of the world, temperature is measured in degrees **Celsius**. In the United States, they measure temperature in degrees **Fahrenheit**.

Story by Melinda Thielbar
Pencils and inks by Der-shing Helmer
Colouring by Hi-Fi Design
Lettering by Marshall Dillon

First published in the United Kingdom in 2010 by
Lerner Books,
Dalton House,
60 Windsor Avenue,
London SW19 2RR

Website address: www.lernerbooks.co.uk

This edition was edited for UK publication in 2010

A CIP record for this book is available from the British Library

First published in the United States of America in 2010

Printed in China

JOY IS REALLY GOOD AT KUNG FU.

JOY WORKS REALLY HARD AT KUNG FU.

SHE'S BEEN SIFU'S STUDENT SINCE SHE WAS YOUR AGE, MICHELLE.

SHE COMES TO CLASS EVERY DAY, EVEN DURING THE HOLIDAYS.

NOT EVERYONE HAS *TIME* TO COME EVERY DAY, SAM.

I DON'T THINK JOY HAS MORE TIME THAN WE DO. I THINK SHE JUST DOES KUNG FU WHILE THE REST OF US ARE DOING OTHER THINGS.

IT'S TOO MUCH WORK, SIFU. I'D LIKE YOUR PERMISSION BEFORE I SELL IT.

IT'S YOUR DECISION, FAIZA.

WE HAVE TO MEET THE BUYER AT 21 NORTH JACOBS STREET IN 15 MINUTES. I'LL ASK BRIAN TO LOCK UP.

I THINK FAIZA'S SELLING THE SCHOOL.

SHE'S GOING WITH SIGUNG TO MEET A BUYER *RIGHT NOW.*

I'LL SEE YOU NEXT TIME, CHILDREN!

BYE, SIFU!

SIGUNG IS SIFU'S KUNG FU TEACHER. SHE SAID SHE NEEDED HIS PERMISSION. WHAT ELSE COULD SHE BE SELLING?

YOU MUST HAVE HEARD THEM TALKING ABOUT SOMETHING ELSE.

SHE WOULDN'T DO THAT.

I THINK I KNOW HOW TO FIND OUT. YOU GUYS FINISH TIDYING UP.

WOULD SHE?

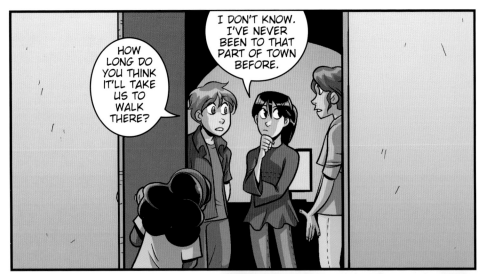

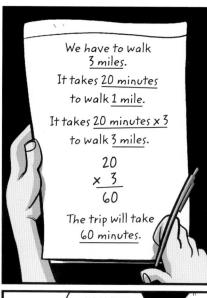

SO YOU SPIED ON YOUR TEACHER, AND NOW YOU WANT TO INTERRUPT HER AT A PRIVATE MEETING?

WE DIDN'T MEAN TO SPY!

WE WERE TRYING TO TAKE OUT THE RUBBISH.

IT'S NOT NICE TO LISTEN IN ON OTHER PEOPLE'S CONVERSATIONS, EVEN ACCIDENTALLY.

IF I GIVE EVERYONE A LIFT HOME AGAIN TODAY, WE'LL PASS BY THAT ADDRESS ON THE WAY TO STACY'S HOUSE. IF WE SEE SIFU FAIZA, WE'LL STOP AND YOU CAN APOLOGIZE FOR EAVESDROPPING.

THAT HOUSE IS HUGE.

THE PERSON BUYING THE SCHOOL MUST BE RICH.

DID THE BUYER ALREADY LEAVE?

THERE'S SIFU'S CAR!

U-TAKE MOVING TRAILERS

AND HOW DO YOU KNOW ABOUT IT?

WE HEARD YOU AND SIGUNG TALKING ABOUT SELLING SOMETHING.

WE THOUGHT YOU WERE TALKING ABOUT THE SCHOOL.

YOU SHOULD HAVE TALKED TO ME.

WE'RE SORRY.

I THINK SORRY ISN'T ENOUGH.

SIFU, WE SHOULDN'T HAVE LISTENED TO YOUR PRIVATE CONVERSATION, AND WE SHOULDN'T HAVE JUMPED TO CONCLUSIONS. HOW CAN WE MAKE IT UP TO YOU?

SIGUNG AND I DO HAVE A LOT OF WORK TO DO HERE. YOU CAN HELP US.

WE CAN DO THAT.

SURE!

FIRST, ALL OF YOU CALL YOUR PARENTS AND ASK FOR PERMISSION.

SIFU SAID SHE'D DRIVE US BACK TO THE KUNG FU SCHOOL IN 3 HOURS, AND IT TAKES 5 MINUTES TO DRIVE THERE.

SO . . . CAN YOU PICK ME UP AT 5:20?

SIFU, IS YOUR THERMOMETER BROKEN?

I THOUGHT 32 DEGREES WAS FREEZING. YOUR THERMOMETER SAYS IT'S 21 DEGREES, BUT IT'S NOT COLD IN HERE.

ON THE **FAHRENHEIT SCALE**, 32 DEGREES IS THE TEMPERATURE WHERE WATER FREEZES. YOU'RE READING THE CELSIUS SIDE OF THE THERMOMETER.

ON THE **CELSIUS SCALE**, WATER FREEZES AT 0 DEGREES, SO 21 DEGREES CELSIUS IS THE TEMPERATURE OF A WARM ROOM. THAT'S ABOUT 70 DEGREES FAHRENHEIT.

PEOPLE IN THE UNITED KINGDOM NOW USE CENTIGRADE BUT OLDER PEOPLE STILL PREFER FAHRENHEIT. WHEN YOU READ A TEMPERATURE, YOU SHOULD CHECK WHICH SCALE IS BEING USED.

NOW, HAVE ALL OF YOU CALLED YOUR PARENTS?

YES, SIFU!

IF NO ONE NEEDS A LIFT, I'LL BE LEAVING. SAM AND MICHELLE, I'LL SEE YOU AT THE KUNG FU SCHOOL IN 3 HOURS.

OK, DAD. THANK YOU FOR THE LIFT.

YOU CAN HELP US PACK BOXES INTO THE VAN.

HI, KIDS! I DIDN'T KNOW YOU WERE HELPING US TODAY.

THEY OFFERED TO CARRY SOME BOXES FOR US.

. . . THE REALLY HEAVY ONES.

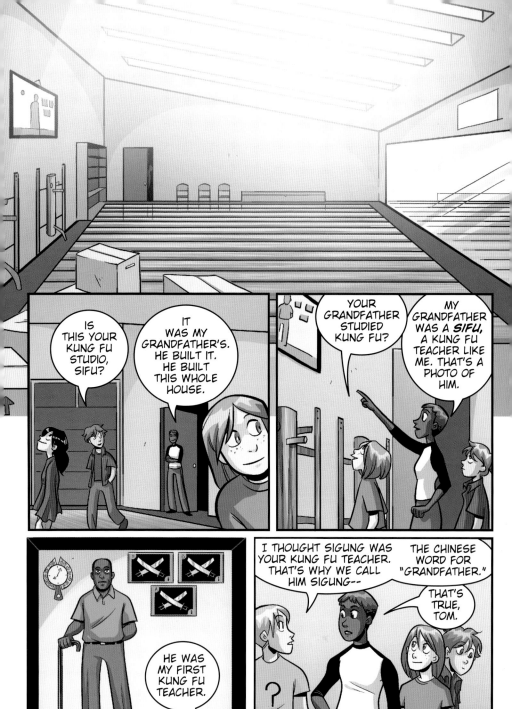

IS THIS YOUR KUNG FU STUDIO, SIFU?

IT WAS MY GRANDFATHER'S. HE BUILT IT. HE BUILT THIS WHOLE HOUSE.

YOUR GRANDFATHER STUDIED KUNG FU?

MY GRANDFATHER WAS A *SIFU*, A KUNG FU TEACHER LIKE ME. THAT'S A PHOTO OF HIM.

HE WAS MY FIRST KUNG FU TEACHER.

I THOUGHT SIGUNG WAS YOUR KUNG FU TEACHER. THAT'S WHY WE CALL HIM SIGUNG--

THE CHINESE WORD FOR "GRANDFATHER."

THAT'S TRUE, TOM.

MY SIFU, YOUR SIGUNG, WAS GRANDFATHER'S *DISCIPLE.* A "DISCIPLE" IS A SPECIAL KIND OF STUDENT.

MY GRANDFATHER BECAME VERY ILL RIGHT AFTER I STARTED LEARNING KUNG FU. HE DIED WHEN I WAS STILL A LITTLE GIRL.

AFTER MY GRANDFATHER WAS GONE . . .

. . . SIFU BECAME MY TEACHER.

AND NOW THAT I'M SELLING THE HOUSE, I'M GOING TO TAKE MY GRANDFATHER'S KUNG FU BOOKS AND HIS WOODEN DUMMIES BACK TO OUR SCHOOL.

WE'LL BE HERE 3 HOURS. THERE ARE 5 GROUPS OF BOXES, PLUS THE WOODEN DUMMIES. THAT MAKES 6 TASKS. WE HAVE A HALF HOUR TO DO EACH TASK.

FRAGILE

OH NO!

NICE CATCH, JOY! KUNG FU TRAINING IS GOOD FOR YOUR REFLEXES.

I'M SORRY, SIFU. I SHOULDN'T HAVE TRIED TO CARRY THE BOX AND THE CLOCK AT THE SAME TIME.

THAT'S ALL RIGHT, AMY. I SHOULD HAVE PACKED THE CLOCK IN ITS OWN BOX.

SIFU, ISN'T THIS CLOCK IN THE PHOTO OF YOUR GRANDFATHER?

THAT'S RIGHT, JOY.

EVERY KUNG FU SCHOOL NEEDS A CLOCK SO CLASS CAN START AND END ON TIME. THIS ONE USED TO HANG IN MY GRANDFATHER'S STUDIO. NOW I'LL HANG IT UP IN OUR SCHOOL.

I'LL PUT THE CLOCK IN YOUR CAR, FAIZA.

THANK YOU, SIFU. WE'LL PICK UP THE BOOKS.

WHAT'S THIS?

IT'S MY FIRST KUNG FU JOURNAL! I THOUGHT IT WAS LOST FOREVER!

To my granddaughter: The study of kung fu requires a disciplined mind. May these exercises help you train your mind, just as I've taught you to train your body.

Love, Grandpa

"THE STUDY OF KUNG FU REQUIRES A DISCIPLINED MIND.

MAY THESE EXERCISES HELP YOU TRAIN YOUR MIND, JUST AS I'VE TAUGHT YOU TO TRAIN YOUR BODY.

LOVE, GRANDPA"

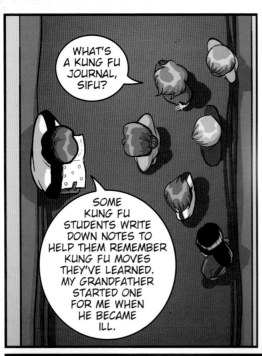

25

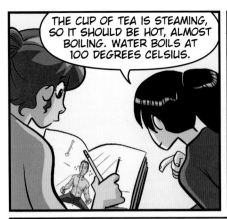

THE CUP OF TEA IS STEAMING, SO IT SHOULD BE HOT, ALMOST BOILING. WATER BOILS AT 100 DEGREES CELSIUS.

I'M NOT SURE ABOUT THAT.

IF WATER BOILS AT 100 DEGREES CELSIUS, THEN WE'D COLOUR 98.6 DEGREES CELSIUS FOR THE CUP OF TEA BECAUSE IT IS HOT, BUT NOT QUITE BOILING.

BUT THAT WOULD MEAN THE MONK HAS A 200-DEGREE TEMPERATURE!

WAIT! I KNOW! MAYBE THE 200 TEMPERATURE AND THE 98.6 TEMPERATURE ARE MEASURED IN DEGREES FAHRENHEIT.

IT WOULD MAKE SENSE FOR THE MONK'S TEMPERATURE TO BE 98.6°F. IF YOU TAKE YOUR TEMPERATURE THE THERMOMETER WILL SAY 37° CELSIUS OR 98.6° FAHRENHEIT WHICH IS NORMAL.

BUT HE'S SWEATING. WOULDN'T HE BE WARMER THAN THAT?

SWEAT IS YOUR BODY'S WAY OF COOLING OFF. WHEN YOU EXERCISE, YOU SWEAT TO KEEP YOUR TEMPERATURE AROUND 98.6°F OR 37°C.

WATER BOILS AT 212°F, SO 200°F WOULD BE RIGHT FOR REALLY *HOT* TEA.

I THINK THAT'S RIGHT, SAM. WHY DON'T YOU COLOR IT IN?

I THINK THE LINE NEXT TO THE THERMOMETER IS FOR WRITING WHETHER THE TEMPERATURE IS IN CELSIUS OR FAHRENHEIT.

YOU SOLVED THE PUZZLE QUICKLY BY WORKING TOGETHER. YOU MAKE A GOOD TEAM.

WE DO, DON'T WE?

NOW YOU'LL WORK TOGETHER TO PACK THE WOODEN DUMMIES ON THE TRUCK. WE'LL NEED TO BE QUICK.

THAT IS STRANGE, TOM. LET'S LOOK AT THE MIDDLE ONE WHEN WE TAKE IT DOWN.

LOOK AT THIS!

MAYBE THE WOODEN DUMMY IS HOLLOW, AND THIS MAKES THE TOP COME OFF.

I DON'T KNOW, MICHELLE.

THIS WOODEN DUMMY WAS MY GRANDFATHER'S. I NEVER USED IT BECAUSE IT WAS SET TOO HIGH FOR ME.

WE'VE TRIED TURNING THE ARM TO EACH POINT ON THE CIRCLE.

SOMETIMES, WHEN YOU'RE STUCK ON A PROBLEM, IT HELPS TO TAKE A BREAK.

LET'S FINISH LOADING THE DUMMIES INTO THE VAN, AND WE'LL THINK ABOUT THIS WHILE WE'RE DRIVING TO THE SCHOOL.

SIFU, MAY I ASK YOU A QUESTION?

YES, JOY.

YOU'VE LIVED IN THIS HOUSE SINCE YOU WERE A LITTLE GIRL, RIGHT?

THAT'S RIGHT.

THEN WHY ARE YOU SELLING THE HOUSE NOW?

IT'S A BIG HOUSE FOR JUST ONE PERSON, JOY.

A FAMILY SHOULD LIVE HERE. PEOPLE WHO NEED LOTS OF SPACE.

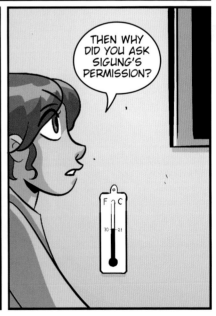

THEN WHY DID YOU ASK SIGUNG'S PERMISSION?

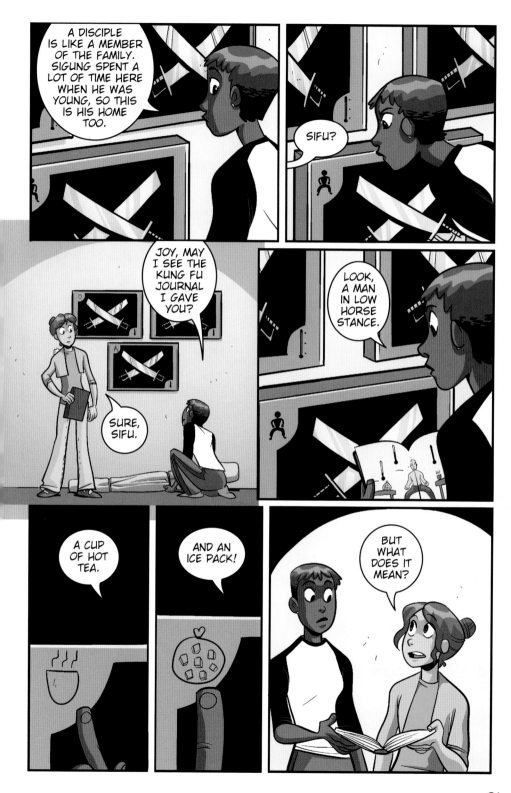

WE'LL PUT THE DUMMIES ON THE FLOOR FOR NOW AND HANG THEM UP ONCE WE'VE FINISHED WITH THE BOXES.

I THOUGHT THAT WAS TOO MANY BOOKS FOR THIS ROOM.

YOU COULD HAVE SAID SO.

BUT GOOD TEACHERS HELP STUDENTS LEARN FOR THEMSELVES.

WHAT KIND OF PUZZLE IS THIS?

4:38 Better
12:47 Minutes
10:02 Twice
3:13 Six
9:01 Five

IS _____ THAN

OH! IT'S LIKE A WORD SCRAMBLE. YOU'RE SUPPOSED TO MATCH THE WORDS WITH THE CLOCKFACE THAT HAS THE RIGHT TIME.

THE FIRST CLOCKFACE SAYS 3:13, SO THE WORD *SIX* GOES FIRST.

I SEE. THE SECOND CLOCKFACE SAYS 12:47, SO **MINUTES** IS THE SECOND WORD.

THE NEXT-TO-LAST CLOCK IS 12:47 TOO, SO **MINUTES** IS IN THE SENTENCE TWICE.

six ___ minutes

is ___ THAN

BETTER IS THE NEXT WORD AFTER **IS**.

THE NEXT CLOCKFACE SAYS 9:01, SO **FIVE** COMES AFTER **THAN**.

ONE LAST CLOCK.

4:38 Better
12:47 Minutes
10:02 Twice
3:13 Six
9:01 Five

six ___ minutes

is better THAN

five minutes

SPEAKING OF TIME, DO YOU THINK WE HAVE TIME TO FINISH PUTTING THE WOODEN DUMMIES UP BEFORE YOUR PARENTS GET HERE?

WELL, IN 10 MINUTES, IT WILL BE 5:00. OUR PARENTS ARE SUPPOSED TO PICK US UP AT 5:20.

10 + 20 IS . . .

YOU COULD JUST COUNT BY TENS. 10 MINUTES, 20 MINUTES . . . OUR PARENTS WILL BE HERE IN 30 MINUTES!

THAT'S A HALF HOUR. IS IT ENOUGH TIME, SIFU?

IT WILL BE IF WE WORK TOGETHER.

WE TRIED POINTING TO EVERY MARK ON THE CIRCLE, AND NOTHING HAPPENED.

WE NEVER DID WORK OUT WHY THIS DUMMY WAS DIFFERENT FROM THE OTHERS.

DID YOU TRY TURNING THE DIAL ALL THE WAY AROUND?

NO! THAT HAS TO BE IT.

THE CIRCLE LOOKS LIKE A CLOCKFACE, AND THE METAL PART REMINDS ME OF A SECOND HAND.

I THINK YOU NEED TO TURN IT SIX TIMES-- *WITHOUT STOPPING.* SO YOU DON'T GO INTO *REST MODE.*

POP!

IT'S FOR YOU, SIFU.

Dear Faiza,

If you've reached this far, you know there are many secrets hidden in our kung fu studio. Be observant, and you will learn them all. If you get stuck, you can always ask your fellow students to help you.

No matter how grown-up you are, there will always be things you don't know.

Love,
Grandpa

WHAT DOES IT SAY, SIFU?

IT SAYS I CAN'T SELL MY GRAND-FATHER'S HOUSE.

DOES THAT MEAN WE HAVE TO MOVE ALL THOSE BOOKS AGAIN?

HaHaHa
HaHaHa
HaHaHa

I HAVE A BETTER IDEA.

THE NEXT DAY.

U-TAKE
MOVING TRAILERS

HELLO, CLASS! WELCOME TO YOUR NEW KUNG FU SCHOOL.

TODAY YOU'RE GOING TO LEARN A NEW KUNG FU TERM, *SI JEE*, WHICH MEANS, "OLDER SISTER."

YOUR SI JEE, JOY, IS GOING TO LEAD THE FORM TODAY.

42

=GULP=
YES,
SIFU.

SHE'S
REALLY
GOOD.

YES,
SHE
IS.

BYE SIFU!

GOOD-BYE, CHILDREN. I'LL SEE YOU NEXT TIME.

SIFU, I THINK I COULD HAVE DONE THE FORM BETTER TODAY, BUT I DIDN'T KNOW I WAS GOING TO LEAD ALL BY MYSELF.

I WASN'T READY!

EVERYONE DOES BETTER WHEN THEY'RE PREPARED. BUT HANDLING SURPRISES IS PART OF LEARNING KUNG FU.

IF YOU EVER NEED TO USE YOUR KUNG FU, IT WILL BE A SURPRISE AND IT WILL BE MUCH SCARIER THAN LEADING A FORM IN FRONT OF YOUR CLASS.

THAT'S TRUE, I GUESS.

NOW, YOU'LL BE MORE READY THE NEXT TIME SOMETHING UNEXPECTED HAPPENS.

OK!

NEXT TIME?

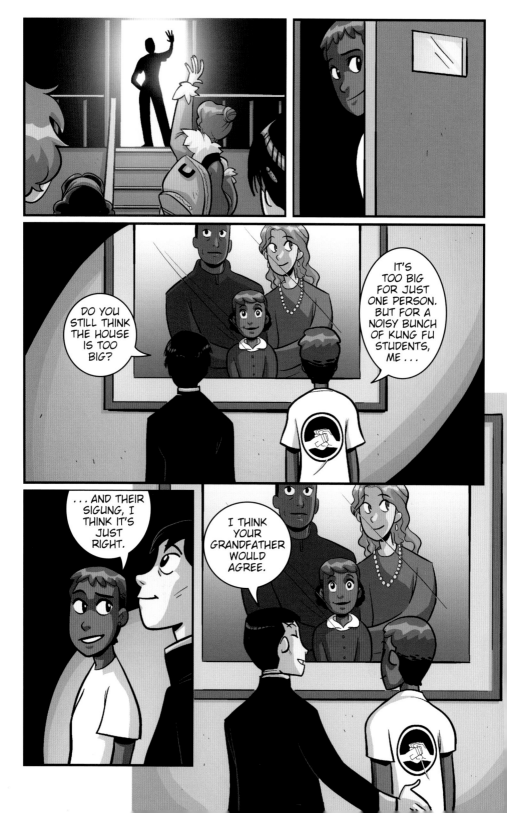

THE END

46

The Author

Melinda Thielbar is a teacher who has written maths courses for all ages, from kids to adults. In 2005 Melinda was awarded a VIGRE fellowship at North Carolina State University for PhD candidates "likely to make a strong contribution to education in mathematics." She lives in Raleigh, North Carolina, with her husband, author and video game programmer Richard Dansky, and their two cats.

The Artists

Tintin Pantoja was born in Manila in the Philippines. She received a degree in illustration and cartooning from the School of Visual Arts in New York City and was nominated for the Friends of Lulu "Best Newcomer" award. She was also a finalist in Tokyopop's Rising Stars of Manga 5. Her past books include a graphic novel version for kids of Shakespeare's play *Hamlet*.

Yuko Ota graduated from the Rochester Institute of Technology and lives in Maryland. She has worked as an animator and a lab assistant but is happiest drawing creatures and inventing worlds. She likes strong tea, the smell of new tyres, and polydactyl cats (cats with extra toes!). She doesn't have any pets, but she has seven houseplants named Blue, Wolf, Charlene, Charlie, Roberto, Steven, and Doris.

Der-shing Helmer graduated with a degree in biology from UC Berkeley, where she played with snakes and lizards all summer long. She is working towards becoming a biology teacher. When she is not coaching kids, she likes to create art, especially comics. Her best friends are her two pet geckos (Smeg and Jerry), her king snake (Clarice), and the chinchilla that lives next door.

ADAM
BY DER-SHING

START READING FROM THE OTHER SIDE OF THE BOOK!

This page would be the first page of a manga from Japan. This is because written Japanese is read from the right side of the page to the left side of the page.

English is read from left to right, so this is the last page of this Manga Maths Mystery. If you read the end of the book first, you'll spoil the mystery! Turn the book over so you can start on the first page. Then find the clues to the mystery with the kids from the kung fu school.

JOIN THE KIDS FROM THE KUNG FU SCHOOL IN SOLVING ALL THE MANGA MATHS MYSTERIES!

ART BY TINTIN PANTOJA

MANGA MATHS MYSTERIES

THE LOST KEY A Mystery with Whole Numbers
THE SECRET GHOST A Mystery with Distance and Measurement
THE KUNG FU PUZZLE A Mystery with Time and Temperature